Walking
With
God

●

Are You a Partner?

Walking
With
God

Are You a Partner?

**Enoch
Adejare
Adeboye**

An imprint of Pneuma Life Publishing
Largo, MD

Christian Living Books, Inc.
An imprint of Pneuma Life Publishing, Inc.
P. O. Box 7584
Largo, MD 20792
301-218-9092
www.christianlivingbooks.com

ISBN 0-9711760-2-7

Printed in the United States of America

Contents

Preface

Taking a walk usually implies choosing a destination and working toward it. Walking with someone else creates a kind of partnership. When you walk before someone, they see all the moves you make and can act as a support in reaching your destination.

God told Abraham to walk before Him in a partnership, with God being the senior partner. After all, He created all things, He is the Almighty and He has the final say.

As a junior partner, you are to fear Him, walk in His ways, love, serve and praise Him. You are to work hard and be ready to give an account of all the assignments given to you by God. You will find that, as soon as He hands out your assignments, the means by which to bring them to pass will be made available. However, in this partnership—just as God told Moses—you must be ready to be absolutely perfect and remain steadfast till the end. If you are upright with God, He will support you and will always be there as your reliable "rear guard."

It is our humble conviction that this book will be a source of inspiration to all Christians, especially ministers of God who are ready to go into partnership with Him.

God bless you.

— Pastor E. A. Adeboye

ONE

Walking Before God

●

When Abram was ninety-nine years old, the LORD appeared to him and said, "I am God Almighty; walk before me and be blameless. (Genesis 17:1)

When you decide to walk, it's usually because you want to get somewhere. The walk must lead to a destination. For example, Paul said:

> *Therefore I do not run like a man running aimlessly; I do not fight like a man beating the air.*
>
> (1 Corinthians 9:26)

In other words, Paul had a goal. To walk, you must have a goal, one you have seen with either the physical eye or the spiritual eye (often called the mind's eye). When I travel, I visualize my destination through the eye of the mind before I start the journey.

All these people were still living by faith when they died. They did not receive the things promised; they only saw them and welcomed them from a distance. And they admitted that they were aliens and strangers on earth. People who say such things show that they are looking for a country of their own. If they had been thinking of the country they had left, they would have had opportunity to return. Instead, they were longing for a better country, a heavenly one. Therefore God is not ashamed to be called their God, for he has prepared a city for them. (Hebrews 11:13-16)

Abraham, Isaac and Jacob all saw their destinies from afar. We too can see far away, namely where we are going to end. You can see Heaven in your mind's eye.

The person walking toward a destination must be willing to reach that goal. Not everyone is. You must believe that the destination *can* be reached. What motivates those who want to reach their objective? It may be to achieve some change in status or for the comfort that the goal brings. Jesus' motivation model can be found in Hebrews:

Let us fix our eyes on Jesus, the author and perfecter of our faith, who for the joy set before him endured the cross, scorning its shame, and sat down at the right hand of the throne of God. (Hebrews 12:2)

Jesus endured the cross to earn the Name above all names. He knew the cost and he knew the good that would come from His sacrifice. It helps to imagine the benefits that come once our goal is reached. Those who strive must count the cost of reaching their objective and be willing to pay the price. For example, if it is raining and you need to reach an adjacent building through the rain, you must be willing to get wet. You will have to weigh getting wet against the importance of the mission you need to accomplish next door.

Walking With God

Suppose one of you wants to build a tower. Will he not first sit down and estimate the cost to see if he has enough money to complete it? For if he lays the foundation and is not able to finish it, everyone who sees it will ridicule him, saying, "This fellow began to build and was not able to finish." (Luke 14:28-30)

It is a glorious thing to be God's favorite, but if you go through the Scriptures, you will discover that it is His favorites that God chastises the most. For example, the way He deals with Israel is different from the way He deals with all other nations of the world. Therefore, once you become His favorite, you had better be upright because you are under His strict supervision. Those of us willing to reach our goals must be willing to fast, pray and study the word of God. We must live in a holy manner and be in absolute obedience to God.

After counting the cost and finding yourself willing, you must then put your efforts into walking. Many people think they are willing but never make any effort. They want to enjoy well-being without the work.

The prodigal son in Luke 15:11-19 made the effort to go back home. Images of the servants in his father's house having a feast crowded his mind while he starved. He knew that going home would bring him shame but he reckoned only the living have an ego as well as a body to feed. He was willing to go home and made the effort, and he had counted the cost before making up his mind.

Even before we make the effort to walk, we first must stand. The next thing is to take a step, then step after step. Do not stop until the destination is reached—something that often requires patience. The writer of Hebrews encourages us:

*Therefore, since we are surrounded by such a great cloud
of witnesses, let us throw off everything that hinders and
the sin that so easily entangles, and let us run with per-
severance the race marked out for us. (Hebrews 12:1)*

Partnership With God

Walk before me and be blameless. (Genesis 17.1)

"Before me" means that there is a partnership between
you and God; the two of you are on a journey. You are
walking in front as the junior partner and He is right
behind you as the senior partner. The apostle Paul put it
this way:

*For we are God's fellow workers; you are God's field,
God's building.* (1 Corinthians 3:9)

And in Matthew, Jesus Christ said:

*Take my yoke upon you and learn from me, for I am
gentle and humble in heart, and you will find rest for
your souls. For my yoke is easy and my burden is light.*
(Matthew 11:29-30)

He says that His yoke is easy because He is already car-
rying the burden. You must never forget that God is the
senior partner and you are the junior partner in your rela-
tionship with Him.

You may say you will never forget that, but when you
begin to succeed, when miracles begin to happen
through you, it's easy to think that you are an equal partner. God forbid that your amnesia ever gets to the stage
where you think that without *you* He will not be able to
do what *He* wants to do! If that time comes, try to remember that He never said "walk beside me" but "walk before

me." You will never be God's equal; He will always be the senior partner. Colossians should remind you:

> *For by him all things were created: things in heaven and on earth, visible and invisible, whether thrones or powers or rulers or authorities; all things were created by him and for him. He is before all things, and in him all things hold together. And he is the head of the body, the church; he is the beginning and the firstborn from among the dead, so that in everything he might have the supremacy.* (Colossians 1:16-18)

This passage lists several reasons why God is the senior partner; for example, He created all things. You can only be His equal if you can say that you created all things. When you begin to create mountains, seas and animals with the word of your mouth, *then* you can say that you are equal with God.

We are also told that all things were created for Him and not for you. This Kingdom to which He has invited you as a partner was created by Him and for Him. By his grace are you allowed to share in it. He is also before all things, far older than you are. He is your superior in age and everything else, and it is He who holds everything in creation together. If you take Him away, everything will disintegrate. Nothing exists outside Him.

God is also the Head of the Body. If you cut off any part of a man's body, he can still live. However, if you cut off the head, that is the end of the story. When the power of God begins to show in your ministry and miracles begin to happen, there will be a strong temptation to dispense with the senior partner. But if you leave Him out, that omission will result in destruction.

Jesus is the beginning and the end. When many of us become successful, we tend to forget the beginning, but a house without a foundation shall surely fall flat. Without Moses, there would have been no Joshua. Without Elijah, there would have been no Elisha.

The Bible text also states that He is the first-born from the dead, the first-born of God. In all the cultures of this world, the first-born is given preference. Lot ended up so badly because he did not let Abraham, a senior relative, choose first where to settle, Jordan or Canaan. (Genesis 13:10-12) Lot forgot that Abraham was the benefactor and that Lot was just a recipient of the blessings.

Because God is the senior partner, He always has the final say. In any partnership, there is somebody who must make the final decision. Without that guidance, it soon becomes disorganized. Whether we like the decision or not, we have to abide by it.

In our own case, we are talking about the Almighty God who can never make mistakes. He knows what we do not know. Let God have the final say in your life; He knows what is best for you. He is the Alpha and the Omega, the beginning and the end. Proverbs presents a good advice:

> Many are the plans in a man's heart, but it is the LORD's purpose that prevails. (Proverbs 19:21)

In a familiar cliché, man proposes but God disposes. Though He may not sack you if you are walking with Him, He can lay you aside or ignore you because He is the senior partner. Paul published a reminder in his letter to the Church in Corinth:

> I beat my body and make it my slave so that after I have preached to others, I myself will not be disqualified for the prize. (1 Corinthians 9:27)

People may still call you "pastor" even though God may have discarded you like yesterday's breakfast gone bad.

King Saul was still on the throne though God had abandoned him long before. But if you behave wisely, then Heaven is your only limit. You cannot begin to imagine how much God will promote you if you are a good partner. A *real* promotion lies in the manifestation of the gifts of the Holy Spirit and not in name or status.

In the Bible, we are told that Deacon Stephen performed signs and wonders among the disciples. They never called him an apostle but I am sure that the apostles respected him. Real promotion is not in names. There might be some workers in the church far higher in God's spiritual reckoning than their pastor.

> *Humble yourselves, therefore, under God's mighty hand,*
> *that he may lift you up in due time.* (1 Peter 5:6)

The length of his arms and probably his legs determines how far a man can lift you up. It's a different thing entirely when the Almighty God lifts you up, because He is the only One who sits on His throne in Heaven and the earth is His footstool. You can imagine the length of His arms by considering the length of His legs (Isaiah 66:1). When He picks you up, you are Heaven-bound in all that concerns you. This is why the Bible states that He gives grace to the humble (James 4:6).

 Remember that no laziness is allowed in your walk with God. He will monitor your activities as you walk before Him.

> *Jesus said to them, "My Father is always at his work to*
> *this very day, and I, too, am working."* (John 5:17)

If the senior partner is working hard, non-stop, then you must also. Spiritual leaders should know that their followers are watching them. If we are hardworking, the people of God will be compelled to work hard. His grace will be sufficient for us and we cannot afford to be lazy. God wants to work through you. The Bible says of Jesus:

> *He was in the world, and though the world was made through him, the world did not recognize him.*
>
> (John 1:10)

> *Do you see a man skilled in his work? He will serve before kings; he will not serve before obscure men.*
>
> (Proverbs 22:29)

God has a way of rewarding your hard work, whether people see you or not. He will make sure you stand before kings if you are really hardworking. But if you are slothful and you are a good propagandist, God has a supernatural way of making sure that you end up before mean men and never stand before kings. Why?

> *One who is slack in his work is brother to one who destroys.* (Proverbs 18:9)

God hates idleness. If you are not working hard then you are a great waster. The apostle Paul repeats the need to be diligent:

> *Never be lacking in zeal, but keep your spiritual fervor, serving the Lord.* (Romans 12:11)

Do any assignment that you are given with all your strength. Time equals life, and time wasted means life wasted. Any day that is not usefully spent for the Lord is a fraction of your life squandered. Let there be no more laziness in your life.

Finally, our senior partner pays well. We cannot find a better partner than the Lord Jesus Christ. He pays with money, divine health, strength, wisdom and, if you really want it, He can pay you with popularity.

The lions may grow weak and hungry, but those who seek the LORD lack no good thing. (Psalm 34:10)

For the LORD God is a sun and shield; the LORD bestows favor and honor; no good thing does he withhold from those whose walk is blameless. (Psalm 84:11)

He will not only pay you but also your children.

I was young and now I am old, yet I have never seen the righteous forsaken or their children begging bread.
(Psalm 37:25)

When it is time for you to retire, He will send His chariots to bring you home.

As they were walking along and talking together, suddenly a chariot of fire and horses of fire appeared and separated the two of them, and Elijah went up to heaven in a whirlwind. (2 Kings 2:11)

Do not let your hearts be troubled. Trust in God; trust also in me. In my Father's house are many rooms; if it were not so, I would have told you. I am going there to prepare a place for you. And if I go and prepare a place for you, I will come back and take you to be with me that you also may be where I am. (John 14:1-3)

He has provided a beautiful retirement home for you. It is worthwhile being in partnership with Jesus Christ; it is a tremendous privilege.

TWO

The Junior Partner

●

When there are two partners in a business, they each have to define their responsibilities. Our duties in our partnership with God can be divided into two major sections: basic and secondary.

Our basic assignments are recorded in Deuteronomy:

> *And now, O Israel, what does the LORD your God ask of you, but to fear the LORD your God, to walk in all his ways, to love him, to serve the LORD your God with all your heart and with all your soul, and to observe the LORD's commands and decrees that I am giving you today for your own good?*
> (Deuteronomy 10:12-13)

> *He is your praise; he is your God, who performed for you those great and awesome wonders you saw with your own eyes. Your forefathers who went down into*

Egypt were seventy in all, and now the LORD your
God has made you as numerous as the stars in the sky.
(Deuteronomy 10:21-22)

We start off in the right direction by fearing Him. *The fear of the Lord is the beginning of wisdom* (Proverbs 9:10). You do not begin to be wise at all until you begin to fear God. You cannot know even a little of the power of God without fearing Him. If you witness His power on display, you will tremble, but this is a good kind of fear, one that preserves you. Any child who is fearless is doomed to foolishness, and that can lead to destruction. Remember David said, *"Your rod and your staff, they comfort me."* (Psalm 23:4). God's rod is for correction while His staff is for protection.

Our next responsibility is to accept all His demands. You are to walk in all His ways and not just *some* of His ways. Some of us pray but ignore holiness. Some of us give but do not witness. Some of us study the Bible but do not praise God. We are to do everything expected of a Christian. Nobody is too big before God, the Almighty, to do all His will. It is the person who humbles himself that the Almighty God regards most highly.

Surely we must also love Him. I do not know how this can be difficult for anyone to do! If you think of how much love He has for you, it should be natural to love Him in return. God loves us so much that He gave His only begotten Son. All He wants from you is that you love Him back; nothing is as painful as love that is not reciprocated. It is even more painful when the one you love disappoints you or betrays you. I can understand why Judas Iscariot was not given any chance to repent. You are consorting with Judas Iscariot if you do not return the love of God, and you surely remember his fate.

A natural follow-up to loving Him is serving Him. As you know, it is easy to serve somebody you love and very difficult to serve somebody you do not love. The reason some of us find it difficult to serve God and talk to Him in prayer may be because our love for Him is waning. If you love God, you will do anything for Him.

Next we come to the language of the partnership: praise. You have to praise God at all times. Looking at the world's state of affairs, some may wonder—what is there to praise God for? We can praise Him for who He is. Some people praise God for houses, properties, cars and clothes, but those who really know God praise Him because He is God. Thank God for Jesus. Thank God for the Holy Spirit. You will always have something to praise God for if God is your praise. Nothing else will matter if you remember that.

In conclusion, everything you do for Him must be with all your heart. You are to fear Him, serve Him, walk in all His ways, love Him and praise Him. Do everything you do for Him joyfully.

> *When the princes in Israel take the lead, when the people willingly offer themselves—praise the LORD!*
> (Judges 5:2)
>
> *I desire to do your will, O my God; your law is within my heart.* (Psalm 40:8)

Everything that you do for God without joy is a waste. The Bible states that God loves a cheerful giver (2 Corinthians 9:7). If you do things the way He says you should, the results will be supernatural. The mere thought of how much He loves you should be enough motivation for you to do things for Him joyfully. Some of us find joy in serving God because, when we look back to our beginnings and the rubble from which He rescued us, we realize it is a joy to serve Him.

Secondary Assignments

God wants you to work hard; He does not like lazy people:

> *"But now be strong, O Zerubbabel," declares the LORD. "Be strong, O Joshua son of Jehozadak, the high priest. Be strong, all you people of the land," declares the LORD, "and work. For I am with you,"'declares the LORD Almighty.* (Haggai 2:4)

I personally encourage you to be strong and work hard. Anything else isn't worth your while. My testimony is that it is secularly and eternally rewarding. 1 Corinthians issues a challenge:

> *Therefore, my dear brothers, stand firm. Let nothing move you. Always give yourselves fully to the work of the Lord, because you know that your labor in the Lord is not in vain.* (1 Corinthians 15:58)

You are expected to become addicted to the work of the Lord. From this scripture we learn from the example of saints in the early Church:

> *You know that the household of Stephanas were the first converts in Achaia, and they have devoted themselves to the service of the saints.* (1 Corinthians 16:15)

The Bible states that we are to submit to people who get addicted to the word of the Lord. If you can be addicted to the work of the ministry, other people will be compelled to submit to you.

But you, keep your head in all situations, endure hardship, do the work of an evangelist, discharge all the duties of your ministry. (2 Timothy 4:5)

Do a thorough work for God, with total joy. If you are a pastor, for instance, you need to pay attention to all departments in your church, but you must also concentrate on your own part.

It's like a man going away: He leaves his house and puts his servants in charge, each with his assigned task, and tells the one at the door to keep watch. (Mark 13:34)

Every man has his work for Him marked out. You are not to be "Jack of all trades, master of none." Your portion of the big work will be assigned to you. And do not try to do other people's work for them. That's the way to keep out of trouble. Our mentor should be the woman who spent both her money and herself to bless Jesus:

While he was in Bethany, reclining at the table in the home of a man known as Simon the Leper, a woman came with an alabaster jar of very expensive perfume, made of pure nard. She broke the jar and poured the perfume on his head. Some of those present were saying indignantly to one another, "Why this waste of perfume? It could have been sold for more than a year's wages and the money given to the poor." And they rebuked her harshly. "Leave her alone," said Jesus. "Why are you bothering her? She has done a beautiful thing to me. The poor you will always have with you, and you can help them any time you want. But you will not always have me. She did what she could. She poured perfume on my body beforehand to prepare for my burial. I tell you the truth, wherever the gospel is preached throughout the world, what she has done will also be told, in memory of her." (Mark 14:3-9)

The Junior Partner

Always see your work through, with no half measures, and complete the work step by step. John explains Jesus' heart on the matter.

> *"My food," said Jesus, "is to do the will of him who sent me and to finish his work."* (John 4:34)

Make sure you finish whatever God gives you to do. Paul makes his unequivocal personal motivation public:

> *However, I consider my life worth nothing to me, if only I may finish the race and complete the task the Lord Jesus has given me—the task of testifying to the gospel of God's grace.* (Acts 20:24)

> *I have fought the good fight, I have finished the race, I have kept the faith.* (2 Timothy 4:7)

Your salvation is a serious affair, so don't joke with it. Philippians adds some passion to this affair:

> *Therefore, my dear friends, as you have always obeyed—not only in my presence, but now much more in my absence continue to work out your salvation with fear and trembling.* (Philippians 2:12)

Special Notes

To whom much is given, much is required.

> *But the one who does not know and does things deserving punishment will be beaten with few blows. From everyone who has been given much, much will be demanded; and from the one who has been entrusted with much, much more will be asked.* (Luke 12:48)

If God gives you a big assignment, He will require big results. If God sends you to a seemingly insignificant place and you follow through on your basic and second-ary assignments in that position, you will be honored just as He will honor someone who was given a whole nation to pastor.

On the Day of Judgment, the pastor of a hundred people will be examined on the life of every Member of his church after his own life has been examined. If he is cleared on the hundred and nobody qualified for hell then he can be sure that he has made Heaven. But if one out of the hundred should stumble because of him, according to the word of God, he is not going to Heaven. If one stumbles because of you it's better for you to drown. (Matthew 18:6-7)

Heaven is out of bounds to a minister of God who sends his followers to hell because of his involvement in forni-cation or other sinful behavior. Do all things to the glory of God.

> *If anyone speaks, he should do it as one speaking the very words of God. If anyone serves, he should do it with the strength God provides, so that in all things God may be praised through Jesus Christ. To him be the glory and the power for ever and ever. Amen.*
>
> (1 Peter 4:11)

In all that you do, the glorification of God must be your goal. Whether you are in the choir, the Sunday school department or a pastor, there must be only one thing paramount in your mind: God's glory. Before you do any-thing, you have to ask whether God will be glorified or not. This will help your decision-making process.

Remember that those who sow in tears reap in joy. Remember that weeping may remain for a night but joy comes in the morning (Psalm 30:5). Remember that only special people are called to become God's partners. If

God has chosen you, you must be ready for both the pleasures and the pains; the tears as well as the laughter; the tiredness, the misunderstandings; even the absolute ingratitude of the people that you are called to serve.

Always remember that the One who made Heaven and Earth was crucified on the tree that He created, by the very men that He created, and He wept at the garden of Gethsemane. A typical night is a mixed bag of confusion, emptiness, darkness, sorrow and tears, but in the morning, there will be light, joy and victory. One day, we will arrive at the place where there will be no more nights.

T H R E E

The Senior Partner

●

When going into partnership with someone, you will definitely want to know what type of person he or she is. This determines whether or not you will enter into the partnership. In discussing the senior partner, we will want to know who God is. We want to know what He has and what He can do.

God introduced Himself to Abraham in Genesis 17:1: *"I am God Almighty."*

Our senior partner is the Almighty God. What exactly do we mean by "Almighty?" If you break the word down you have "All" and "Mighty." This means the One who has all might. If you relate to God as the One who has all power, He will show you His power. If you relate to Him as the One who can do all things, He will show you that He surely can do all things.

When you say that He is your healer, He will want to find out whether you really mean it. Your healing may not come immediately after you have prayed. He may deliberately want to know if you have faith in His solution and its timing.

Shadrach, Meshach and Abednego boasted of the God they served. They went into the fire completely convinced that He was able to deliver them and that He would deliver them, and they got into the fire. He could have delivered them before that; He could have sent a thunder bolt to wipe out Nebuchadnezzar's army. But He wanted to be sure that they really meant what they said about Him.

Our senior partner, the Almighty, is also called the Most High.

> *He who dwells in the shelter of the Most High will rest in the shadow of the Almighty.* (Psalm 91:1)

The Bible tells us about someone who is higher than the highest:

> *If you see the poor oppressed in a district, and justice and rights denied, do not be surprised at such things; for one official is eyed by a higher one, and over them both are others higher still.* (Ecclesiastes 5:8)

Because God is the Most High, you have nothing to worry about if you are in business with Him. If the highest authority is on your side, you will win every case. You have every reason to be happy to have the Most High as your senior partner. You can always report anyone who wants to stand in your way to Him.

God once directed an angel to reclaim the corpse of Moses. But Satan stood in the way, laying his own claim to the body. The angel simply reported him to the Highest Authority and that settled the matter (Jude v 9). When someone wants to stand in my way, I report the fellow to the Most High. In Daniel, we discover that our Senior Partner is the Sovereign One:

> All the peoples of the earth are regarded as nothing. He does as he pleases with the powers of heaven and the peoples of the earth. No one can hold back his hand or say to him: "What have you done?" (Daniel 4:35)

He does exactly as He pleases, and nobody can challenge His actions. This brings two major facts into focus. First, He does as He pleases so when it seems that He is promoting somebody above you, do not grumble. You cannot challenge Him.

> Remember the former things, those of long ago; I am God, and there is no other; I am God, and there is none like me. I make known the end from the beginning, from ancient times, what is still to come. I say: My purpose will stand, and I will do all that I please.
>
> (Isaiah 46:9-10)

He is God and there is none like Him or besides Him. He settled everything before the beginning of the world. He had declared the end from the beginning. Additionally, whatever may be happening to you is what He has already planned for your life, and what is happening to your neighbors is what He planned for them. If you take your eyes off where He is taking you and you look at where He is taking someone else, you will falter. When God has made up His mind as to what you will become, whether the devil likes it or not, it will be so. He will do all His pleasure.

Our senior partner rules by decree; He only has to speak and it is done. If He has not spoken, things can still be changed. The matter is settled, however, once He has spoken.

Let all the earth fear the LORD; let all the people of the world revere him. For he spoke, and it came to be; he commanded, and it stood firm. The LORD foils the plans of the nations; he thwarts the purposes of the peoples. But the plans of the LORD stand firm forever, the purposes of his heart through all generations. Blessed is the nation whose God is the LORD, the people he chose for his inheritance. (Psalm 33:8-12)

That which is of God can never be overthrown or destroyed. Acts also attests to this everlasting truth:

Therefore, in the present case I advise you: Leave these men alone! Let them go! For if their purpose or activity is of human origin, it will fail. But if it is from God, you will not be able to stop these men; you will only find yourselves fighting against God. (Acts 5:38-39)

What He Has

1 Chronicles gives us a summary of the qualities our senior partner possesses:

Wealth and honor come from you; you are the ruler of all things. In your hands are strength and power to exalt and give strength to all. (1 Chronicles 29:12)

Riches belong to Him and since the work is His, He will supply money for the work to be done. Riches come from Him. Power comes from Him.

God has spoken once, Twice I have heard this: That power belongs to God. (Psalm 62:11 NKJV)

Original and holy power comes from God. Do not go looking for power from another source, nor forget that you should not joke with your salvation. He is the best and ultimate definition of might, the one who makes people great, regardless of their age. Moses did not become great until he was eighty years old. He had lost all hope of greatness but he was given an extra forty years. Greatness comes from God; you cannot make yourself so. Do not join those who boast of dripping with anointing. The truly great are humble, and the humbler you are, the greater you become.

Strength comes from Him. Our senior partner is the one who put the big mountains in their pre-ordained positions.

> *Who formed the mountains by your power, having armed yourself with strength.* (Psalm 65:6)

Finally, dominion belongs to Him. Nobody can query Him if He decides to hand over a country or any other thing to you.

What He Can Do

Even if you go and fight courageously in battle, God can overthrow you before the enemy, for God has the power to help or to overthrow. (2 Chronicles 25:8)

This was the message sent to one of the enemies of God. Nevertheless, there is an operative word there that we need as His children. God has power to *help*. There are some people who have power but cannot help. Our God has the power *and* He can help.

> *I lift up my eyes to the hills—where does my help come from? My help comes from the LORD, the Maker of heaven and earth.* (Psalm 121:1-2)

God also has the power to keep promises. Romans records Abraham's absolute confidence in God:

The Senior Partner

Being fully persuaded that God had power to do what he had promised. (Romans 4:21)

Many people make promises that they cannot keep, but our God is able to keep all his promises. He has both the ability and the grace to get it done.

And God is able to make all grace abound to you, so that in all things, at all times, having all that you need, you will abound in every good work.

(2 Corinthians 9:8)

We need tremendous grace to do all that we are going to do in His vineyard. We need grace to keep us humble and holy. We need grace to help us manage our prosperity so that it will not choke the life of God out of us.

God has the power to do all that we can ask from Him:

Now to him who is able to do immeasurably more than all we ask or imagine, according to his power that is at work within us. (Ephesians 3:20)

And finally, He is able to keep you from falling:

To him who is able to keep you from falling and to present you before his glorious presence without fault and with great joy. (Jude 24)

The Role of Our Senior Partner

The fact that our senior partner has the power to help does not necessarily mean that He *will* help. I may have power to help someone but refuse to help for one reason or the other. But I can assure you that God will help you. The leper came to Him in Matthew 8:1-3 and asked if Jesus was willing to heal him. In other words, he knew that Jesus had the power to cleanse him but he was not

Walking With God

sure that Jesus Christ would be willing. Jesus said He would, and He will help you, too.

> *So do not fear, for I am with you; do not be dismayed, for I am your God. I will strengthen you and help you; I will uphold you with my righteous right hand. All who rage against you will surely be ashamed and disgraced; those who oppose you will be as nothing and perish. Though you search for your enemies, you will not find them. Those who wage war against you will be as nothing at all. For I am the LORD, your God, who takes hold of your right hand and says to you, Do not fear; I will help you. Do not be afraid, O worm Jacob, O little Israel, for I myself will help you," declares the LORD, your Redeemer, the Holy One of Israel. See, I will make you into a threshing sledge, new and sharp, with many teeth. You will thresh the mountains and crush them, and reduce the hills to chaff. You will winnow them, the wind will pick them up, and a gale will blow them away. But you will rejoice in the LORD and glory in the Holy One of Israel. The poor and needy search for water, but there is none; their tongues are parched with thirst. But I the LORD will answer them; I, the God of Israel, will not forsake them. I will make rivers flow on barren heights, and springs within the valleys. I will turn the desert into pools of water, and the parched ground into springs.* (Isaiah 41:10-18)

The Senior Partner

God says you need not fear because He is your senior partner and will strengthen you. He will help us and uphold us with the right hand of His righteousness. God says all the "mountains" in the way of all that is good for us shall be blown away. We will be proud of being connected to the Holy One of Israel, and He will supply the resources we need. God's pledge never to leave or forsake us can be found in Hebrews:

Keep your lives free from the love of money and be content with what you have, because God has said, "Never will I leave you; never will I forsake you. So we say with confidence, "The Lord is my helper; I will not be afraid. What can man do to me?" (Hebrews 13:5-6)

Provided your conversation is without covetousness and you are content with whatever you have, He will then stand by His promise not to leave you or forsake you. It is when He is by your side that you will be able to say that He is your Helper. If you can say this, then you have nothing to fear. God will supply you with the means to achieve any assignment He gives you. When you run into dead ends, you need to check whether you are following His program or your own program. But if you are doing what He asked you to do, He will definitely supply what you need to do it.

The Sovereign LORD has given me an instructed tongue, to know the word that sustains the weary. He wakens me morning by morning, wakens my ear to listen like one being taught. (Isaiah 50:4)

God gives the assignment and supplies the ability and the grace to do it. Do not be afraid. He will not give you an assignment that you cannot handle.

For it is God who works in you to will and to act according to his good purpose. (Philippians 2:13)

He will make you willing and then He will supply the ability to do His will.

May the God of peace, who through the blood of the eternal covenant brought back from the dead our Lord Jesus, that great Shepherd of the sheep, equip you with everything good for doing his will, and may he work in

us what is pleasing to him, through Jesus Christ, to
whom be glory for ever and ever. Amen.

(Hebrews 13:20-21)

He is the one who will do the work.

Then the LORD said to Moses, "Why are you crying
out to me? Tell the Israelites to move on. Raise your staff
and stretch out your hand over the sea to divide the
water so that the Israelites can go through the sea on dry
ground. (Exodus 14:15-16)

Then the word of the LORD came to him, saying, Get
away from here and turn eastward, and hide by the
Brook Cherith, which flows into the Jordan. And it will
be that you shall drink from the brook, and I have com-
manded the ravens to feed you there. So he went and did
according to the word of the LORD, for he went and
stayed by the Brook Cherith, which flows into the
Jordan. The ravens brought him bread and meat in the
morning, and bread and meat in the evening; and he
drank from the brook. (1 Kings 17:2-6 NKJV)

Before commanding Elijah, He had commanded the
ravens to bring him food. He had finished the Garden of
Eden before He created Adam. Even before the brook
dried up in 1 Kings 17:7-16, He had provided for the
widow who continued feeding Elijah.

Moses answered, "What if they do not believe me or lis-
ten to me and say, `The LORD did not appear to
you'?'" Then the LORD said to him, "What is that in
your hand?" "A staff," he replied. The LORD said,
"Throw it on the ground." Moses threw it on the ground
and it became a snake, and he ran from it. Then the
LORD said to him, "Reach out your hand and take it
by the tail." So Moses reached out and took hold of the

snake and it turned back into a staff in his hand... So
Moses took his wife and sons, put them on a donkey and
started back to Egypt. And he took the staff of God in
his hand. (Exodus 4:1-4, 20)

When He sends you to a "pharaoh", He will give you a "rod" of God to show that He sent you. He is not going to give you a brand new rod from Heaven but He will change the rod that you already have to His rod. Your hands will become the hands of God. Your voice will be changed to His voice. People looking at you will see the glory of God in you.

You need to know that God cares. Our senior partner is not a slave driver and will not treat us like slaves. Though He demands hard work from us, it is in a loving and caring way. Don't pass up His promise:

> *For who is God besides the LORD? And who is the*
> *Rock except our God? It is God who arms me with*
> *strength and makes my way perfect. He makes my feet*
> *like the feet of a deer; he enables me to stand on the*
> *heights. He trains my hands for battle; my arms can*
> *bend a bow of bronze. You give me your shield of victo-*
> *ry, and your right hand sustains me; you stoop down to*
> *make me great.* (Psalm 18:31-35)

The gentleness of our God makes us great. He is powerful, yet He cares. When Elijah asked for death, God gave him food, water and rest (1 Kings 19). He chastises but also embraces. There is an interesting story in Joshua:

> *So when the people broke camp to cross the Jordan, the*
> *priests carrying the ark of the covenant went ahead of*
> *them. Now the Jordan is at flood stage all during har-*
> *vest. Yet as soon as the priests who carried the ark*
> *reached the Jordan and their feet touched the water's*
> *edge, the water from upstream stopped flowing. It piled*

*up in a heap a great distance away, at a town called
Adam in the vicinity of Zarethan, while the water flow-
ing down to the Sea of the Arabah (the Salt Sea) was
completely cut off. So the people crossed over opposite
Jericho.* (Joshua 3:14-16)

On this occasion, the Jordan River was overflowing its
banks. As soon as the priests stepped in the river, God
caused dry land to appear. God needs to see you engage
the gear of obedience and He will do the rest.
Furthermore, God allows for mutual respect in this partnership:

> *Though the LORD is on high, he looks upon the lowly,
> but the proud he knows from afar.* (Psalm 138:6)

As exalted as the Most High is, God still respects the
humble. Very few things can create a gap between you
and God faster than pride, and trouble is the heritage of
the proud. Finally, God is a reliable "rear guard." He will
back you up fully and for the whole mile. He does not fall
asleep and cannot be taken by surprise:

> *That is why I am suffering as I am. Yet I am not
> ashamed, because I know whom I have believed, and am
> convinced that he is able to guard what I have entrust-
> ed to him for that day.* (2 Timothy 1:12)

Commit yourself, your family and your future to Him
and He will take care of all of you. Your future is secure
with Jehovah.

The Senior Partner

F O U R

"Be Thou Perfect"

●

How does one walk perfectly? It cannot mean walking sloppily, staggering or dragging the feet. It means walking upright, straight, without stopping, without wobbling, briskly and steadfastly, and not forgetting why you are walking in the first place.

Walk Upright

> *With the merciful thou wilt shew thyself merciful; with an upright man thou wilt shew thyself upright.*
> (Psalm 18:25 KJV)

If you walk honestly in your partnership with God, you will enjoy your partner and the walk because honesty takes its meaning from Him.

> *Good and upright is the LORD; therefore he instructs sinners in his ways.* (Psalm 25:8)

God is an upright God, not a crooked one. Be truthful with God. You cannot afford to play games with Him.

> For the LORD is righteous, he loves justice; upright men will see his face. (Psalm 11:7)

You are an enduring beauty to the eyes of the Lord if you are upright:

> Surely the righteous will praise your name and the upright will live before you. (Psalm 140:13)

If you are upright, you will dwell in God's presence where there is fullness of joy. Fear, sorrow and sadness come when you become dishonest with God. Little wonder then that the Psalmist says:

> The LORD detests the sacrifice of the wicked, but the prayer of the upright pleases him. (Proverbs 15:8)

The prayers of the upright will be heard by Him and answered. Prayer is conversation with God. When you are upright, He will love to talk with you.

> If you are pure and upright, even now he will rouse himself on your behalf and restore you to your rightful place. Your beginnings will seem humble, so prosperous will your future be. (Job 8:6-7)

If you are upright with Him, He will take care of you:

> For the LORD God is a sun and shield; the LORD bestows favor and honor; no good thing does he withhold from those whose walk is blameless. (Psalm 84:11)

> The days of the blameless are known to the LORD, and their inheritance will endure forever. (Psalm 37:18)

Walking With God

Consider the blameless, observe the upright; there is a future for the man of peace. (Psalm 37:37)

Walk Straight

Be straight in your walk with God so you can prosper. Let all you do mirror the word of God.

Do not let this Book of the Law depart from your mouth; meditate on it day and night, so that you may be careful to do everything written in it. Then you will be prosperous and successful. (Joshua 1:8)

Do not be carried away by all kinds of strange teachings. It is good for our hearts to be strengthened by grace, not by ceremonial foods, which are of no value to those who eat them. (Hebrews 13:9)

Have nothing to do with people who change easily, like chameleons, or are fickle. Be like God who is the same yesterday, today and forever.

My son, fear the LORD and the king; Do not associate with those given to change. (Proverbs 24:21 NKJV)

Jesus replied, "No one who puts his hand to the plow and looks back is fit for service in the kingdom of God."
(Luke 9:62)

If you look back while your hands are still on the plow, the plow will not go straight—although He did not say taking your hands off disqualifies you. Once you decide to go along with God as your partner, you are to go in His direction only. Do not backslide.

The eye is the lamp of the body. If your eyes are good, your whole body will be full of light. (Matthew 6:22)

"Be Thou Perfect"

Walk Briskly

There is a time set for everything under Heaven, so do not leave until tomorrow what you can do today.

> *Moses said to the Gadites and Reubenites, "Shall your countrymen go to war while you sit here?*
>
> (Numbers 32:6)

When the other tribes of Israel made ready for war to possess their portion of the Promised Land, the descendants of Reuben and Gad did not want to help them out. They said they were satisfied with their own side of the Jordan. Moses was astounded. He wondered why they wanted to stay back. The children of Gad did not get to the Promised Land and all the demons exiting the land of Canaan took them over.

When the opportunity comes, you have to act quickly. Strike the iron when it's still hot.

> *So Joshua said to the Israelites: "How long will you wait before you begin to take possession of the land that the LORD, the God of your fathers, has given you?*
>
> (Joshua 18:3)

Time waits for no one. I'm sure you want to avoid what Jeremiah warns against:

> *A curse on him who is lax in doing the LORD's work!*
> *A curse on him who keeps his sword from bloodshed!*
>
> (Jeremiah 48:10)

> *Curse Meroz," said the angel of the LORD. "Curse its people bitterly, because they did not come to help the LORD, to help the LORD against the mighty.*
>
> (Judges 5:23)

Meroz stayed back and was cursed. One of the reasons why God cursed Ephraim was that he did not go to battle for God. The work of the King requires urgency.

Walk Steadfastly

> *Therefore, my dear brothers, stand firm. Let nothing move you. Always give yourselves fully to the work of the Lord, because you know that your labor in the Lord is not in vain.* (1 Corinthians 15:58)

How long must you remain steadfast? The answer is in Hebrews:

> *We have come to share in Christ if we hold firmly till the end the confidence we had at first.* (Hebrews 3:14)

> *And they continued steadfastly in the apostles' doctrine and fellowship, in the breaking of bread, and in prayers.*
> (Acts 2:42 NKJV)

Be steadfast in doctrine:

> *I am coming soon. Hold on to what you have, so that no one will take your crown.* (Revelation 3:11)

Endure till the end even though this takes rugged determination. You have to remain steadfast till the end.

"Be Thou Perfect"

About the Author

Enoch Adejare Adeboye became the General Overseer of The Redeemed Christian Church of God in 1981. The church has experienced unprecedented growth since he became its spiritual and administrative head. Under his leadership, the church hosts a monthly prayer vigil on the first Friday of every month at the headquarters in the Redemption Camp, on the outskirts of Lagos, Nigeria, attracting about 500,000 people per session. Similar meetings are held bi-annually in the United Kingdom and the United States, where the Church has a strong presence.

Also in the eighties, God led Pastor Adeboye to establish "model parishes" that continue to bring young people into the Kingdom in large numbers. The church now has over two million members in about four thousand parishes all over the world.

Pastor Adeboye, a mathematician who holds a Ph.D. in hydrodynamics, lectured at the University of Lagos, Nigeria for many years. He is also a prolific writer of many titles used by God to touch lives. He is married to Pastor Foluke Adeboye and they are blessed with four children.